MAD
cars

MAD cars

GILES
CHAPMAN

First published in the United Kingdom in 2002 by
Sutton Publishing Limited exclusively for
WHSmith, Greenbridge Road, Swindon SN3 3LD

British Library Cataloguing in Publication Data
A catalogue record for this book is available from the
British Library.

ISBN 0-7509-3140-X

Typeset in 9.5/13.5pt Helvetica and produced by
Sutton Publishing Limited, Phoenix Mill,
Thrupp, Stroud, Gloucestershire GL5 2BU.
Printed and bound in England by
J.H. Haynes & Co. Ltd, Sparkford.

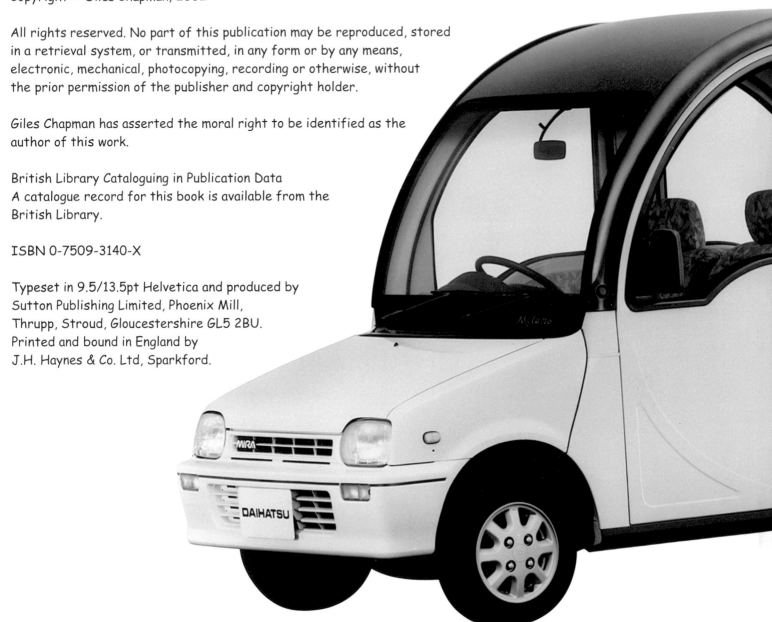

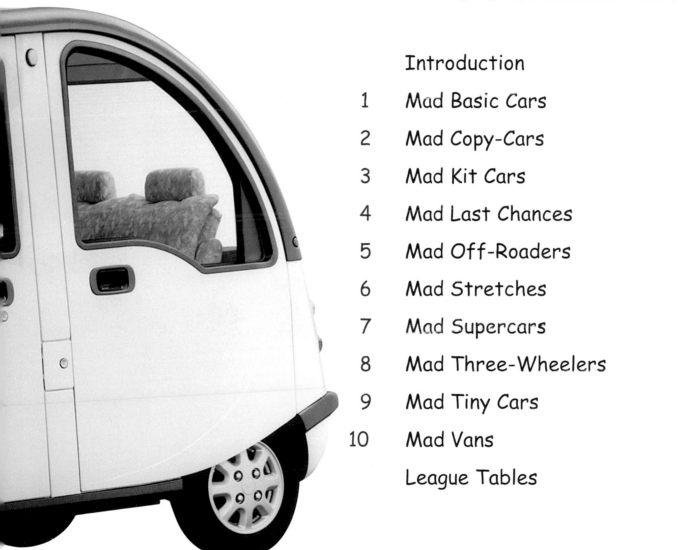

CONTENTS